My Thoughts as a Daughter

Lidia Pifas

BookLeaf Publishing

Presentation by *BookLeaf Publishing*

Web: www.bookleafpub.com

E-mail: info@bookleafpub.com

ISBN: 9789357742283

First edition 2023

ACKNOWLEDGEMENT

Thank you Cici for pushing me to keep writing and for constantly encouraging me.

PREFACE

Inspiration came to me through personal experience. Growing up, I spent many hours alone with my thoughts. Writing was a great way to express how I was feeling in those times. However, this was my first attempt in recapturing my memories through a poem format. While many of the entries follow past reflections, there are a few written as present observations. I had a difficult time finding the words to match my emotions but found myself being able to appreciate the up's and down's in these poems.

My Mother's Silly Rhyme

Life can be crazy, you know what I mean,
hoping around like a jellybean.
It's not my choice, of course,
I am in fact a horse.
Then why is my mother a trampoline?

A Curious Child

Where are we going?
Can't we stay? I like it here.
I want to find home.

Single Mother

Long hours, little reward.
To feed, to clothe, to shelter.
Her goal? To survive.
Always grateful, never ambitious.
the result? Became a shadow,
never seen, but always there.

Lonely Week

Mondays are hard since I won't see her until
Friday.
Out like a light on weekends, she's always so
tired.
Missing her already and it's not even Sunday.

Parents

Who said I didn't have a mom and dad?
If that were true, I'd be quite sad.
But since my mom is mom and dad to me,
I have no reason to not smile with glee.

Moving Away

The numbness I feel is familiar,
as is the blur of my view.
The memories I made were precious,
I'll take them with me someplace new.
This has become routine, not only to me,
but also to my mother and sister, my family.
Planting roots is always promised,
the date just never set.
Hopefully this familiar feeling will fade.
I only ask for my constant to stay.

Going Through Her Head

Don't ask for too much or we'll waste money.
All my friends have so much, I don't think that's
fair.
Until when are we gonna stop moving?
Grandma and grandpa are so nice, but I miss
mommy.
How come dad hasn't come to visit?
Tired of all the fast food we've been eating.
Even though our family's small, I think it's great.
Rent is late again, I wish I could help mom.

Powerless

How can I help you?
Everyday feels like a war.
I don't know what to do.
I am your responsibility, it's true,
but I want to help you do so much more.
How can I help you?
While you were away, I grew.
You said you'd lean on me, you swore.
I don't know what to do.
The payments are past due.
It wasn't this bad before.
How can I help you?
We can't ask for money from you know who.
All this struggle for the children you bore.
I don't know what to do.
I worry you'll fall apart, so I stick to you like
glue.
Don't worry I'll clean up the tears on the floor
How can I help you?
I don't know what to do.

Time Lost

A haze appears as I think of your face.
Small moments turned into puzzle pieces.
Savoring each moment to solve, to chase
the image of you beyond my reaches.
I imagine your eyes strong and steady,
never fading in their comforting light.
In dreams your smile is constantly ready
to warm my heart through a cold winters night.
However, reality calls to me.
Asking to look past the features I seek,
to instead see you as you are truly.
Someone who is kind, loyal, and unique.
Our past remains unchanged, I'm now taller.
Lets find our courage and face each other.

Sisters

Big sister is me,
but I can't take care of her.
We both want our mom.

Farewell Childhood

What a beautiful child.
Their smile leaves impressions on the soul,
with a laughter tickling the ears.
A spirit so free, as if its flying away,
their innocence leave them as light as air.
Away they go without looking back,
a sinking feeling settles in.
They've gone too far from view.
That smile cannot be recalled.
The laughter has become deaf to the ears.
A spirit so free has become a ghost so haunting.
Innocence? what was that?
How close it was to air to be forgotten,
only to be missed when lungs are breathless.

Her Perseverance

A girl who smiles bright
because that's all she can do.
A daughter who wants to be a knight.
She would guard the cries heard at night
and protect the days that seemed so blue.
A girl who smiles bright,
as if to say "everything will be alright",
but uncertainty grew.
A daughter who wants to be a knight,
but she didn't know how to join the fight.
Her resolve began to boil over into stew.
A girl who smiles bright,
hoping to inspire strength and might,
only to be tested each day anew.
A daughter who wants to be a knight
to those in darkness, she wanted to bring light.
A hero with a heart that is true.
A girl who smiles bright.
A daughter who wants to be knight.

Wavering Faith

Oh lord, I pray to thee my king,
that your light may never leave me.
Grant me strength so I may bring
the tools we need to fix this family.
It's just us three in this world,
we have no one else to turn to.
Our lives have been rocked and whirled.
The only way to save us is through you
However my mind can't help but wonder,
I won't lie it feels like doubt.
If you can control the rain and thunder,
how could you let this disaster come about?

The Bitterness Between

The Time we share is unfair.
Always on the move, always on the go.
Never stopping or slowing long enough to show
a smile, your love, a second to care.
The loneliness was hard to bear,
but your troubles weighed you down low.
How was I to know?
Words were unspoken so I would just stare
at the thread that tied us together.
Strained was the string, so thin.
Life has not been kind to us it seems.
Perhaps one day, in calmer weather,
we'll untangle our thoughts within
and enjoy the warm sunbeams.

A Gifted Hope

The greatest honor God has bestowed
is being able to provide to those I love.
No more will I feel helpless.
I have been blessed by those above
to be filled with purpose and joy overflowed.
Finally, we'll be as free as a flying dove.
From now on I'll be fearless,
because my family is taken care of.

A Bigger Painting

Willow trees are often weeping,
their source of sorrow unknown.
While tears are often given,
never is it seen as a gift.
Oh how often we weep as a willow,
choking on our cry's.
Wondering if we should be cut down
to stop this water from running anymore.
Little do we know our tears became a river
that gave life to a dessert.
We were once a tree,
now we are an oasis.

A Need To Be Close

I'm older now mom,
but I want to stay with you.
Lean on me and rest.

Goodnight

Sleep to restore your strength,
dawn approaches in haste.
How long you've tired your bones.
The day challenged you thoroughly.
A blessing when you decided to stay.
Rest to fight off the demons,
the ones who whisper you to go.
To leave the title you've longed for,
abandon what you swore to protect.
How alluring the door seems,
but close your eyes and lay your head.
Tomorrow is a new day.

Unbroken Heart

My   love
for you   is simple.
From start to end it's clear.
This road we walk together
is more precious than silver.
To stay joyful is hard, the
heart often aches,
but the love will
always
stay.

Spotlight

Thankful, grateful, indescribable.
My thoughts and feelings uncontainable.
The greatness that is you
is unshaken in my view.
Here stands a hero
struggling, fighting, surviving.
Quitting was inconceivable.
My love for you immeasurable
Neither exaggeration or imagination
have clouded my judgment.
You, who stayed, shine brightly.
The ones who leave are shadows.

After The End

Imperfection is written within us.
Mistakes are meant to be made.
Our choices flow like streams,
into ponds, into rivers, into oceans.
We can't help but look back.
Regret is the enemy,
of this we learn too late.
But Mistake and Regret
were never our names.
We were a path happily welcomed.
Though the terrain would be rough,
our resolve never broke.
Together we became brave.